Color Your Way to an Anxiety Free Life

Paul Anthony & Melissa Wright

Color Your Way to an Anxiety Free Life

Coloring is a lot of fun – that's why you picked up this program. Coloring also calms the negative effects of your anxiety. And we'll explain everything you need to know to color you way to an anxiety free life.

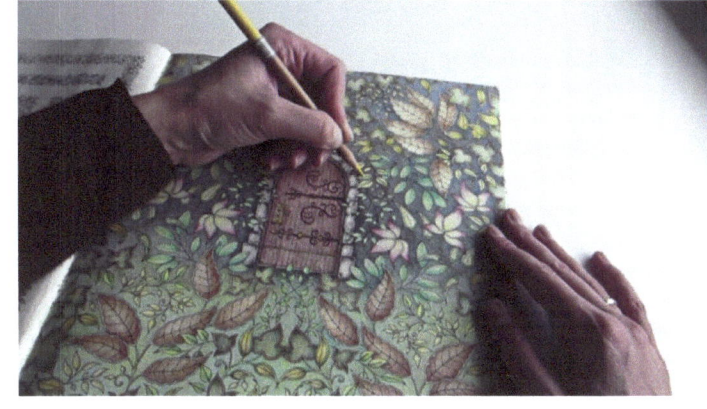

Since you've purchased this program, you've made the first important step in overcoming the anxiety symptoms that have robbed you of countless moments of relaxation, enjoyment and fulfillment.

You deserve what you want out of life – without being hindered by the thoughts and feelings that have been crippling you for months, weeks, even years.

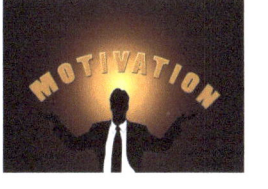

Motivation to change brought you here. And that motivation will help carry you to the next step – curing your anxiety for good.

As we come upon situations in our lives that repeatedly cause us anxiety, our brains create habitual reactions to those situations. Those reactions become so ingrained in our psyche that we reach a point where they become the automatic reaction to the situation, every time it happens.

A problem occurs when the habitual reaction is one that causes us to have anxiety symptoms.

Thinking Errors occur when your automatic thought is distorted by your perspective. You still accept it as true. You've created a maladaptive or dysfunctional automatic thought, also called a cognitive distortion, or simply, a *thinking error*.

You must first become aware of and identify your automatic thoughts or thinking errors. Proactively become aware of what's actually happening in a given situation.

Begin by challenging your automatic thoughts. "What would I tell someone I loved if they were in this situation and had these thoughts?" "If my automatic thought is true, what is the worst that could happen?" "What is the best thing that could happen?"

Using Coloring as a Way to Meditate

Among the hundreds of different relaxation techniques that psychologists, psychotherapists, and other profesionals suggest to their clients, only five are recognized as truly effective:

1. Relaxing the body through alternating muscle tension and muscle relaxation

2. Using hypnosis to increase mental focus/relaxation,

3. Using a autogenic training, which is a form of self-suggestion relaxation,

4. Visualization of pleasant scenes and sensations, and

5. Diaphragmatic breathing (slow belly-breathing).

Coloring incorporates nearly all of the five. The body relaxes as you color. You are hyper focused on your work, which can put the body into a near state of hypnosis. It provides a sense of control over the sit-

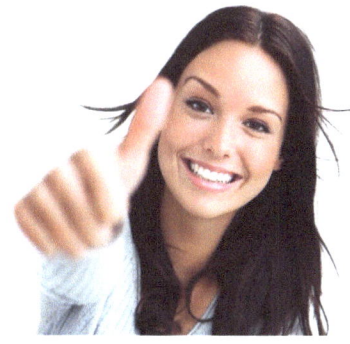

uation in that the person coloring chooses the palette. You create the rules and boundaries, and aren't restricted by outside forces. It's your world. Coloring has a track-record of bringing about a non-anxious state. It uses meditation and distraction in order to bring the body and mind into sync by combining aspects *continued on page 24*

continued on page 24

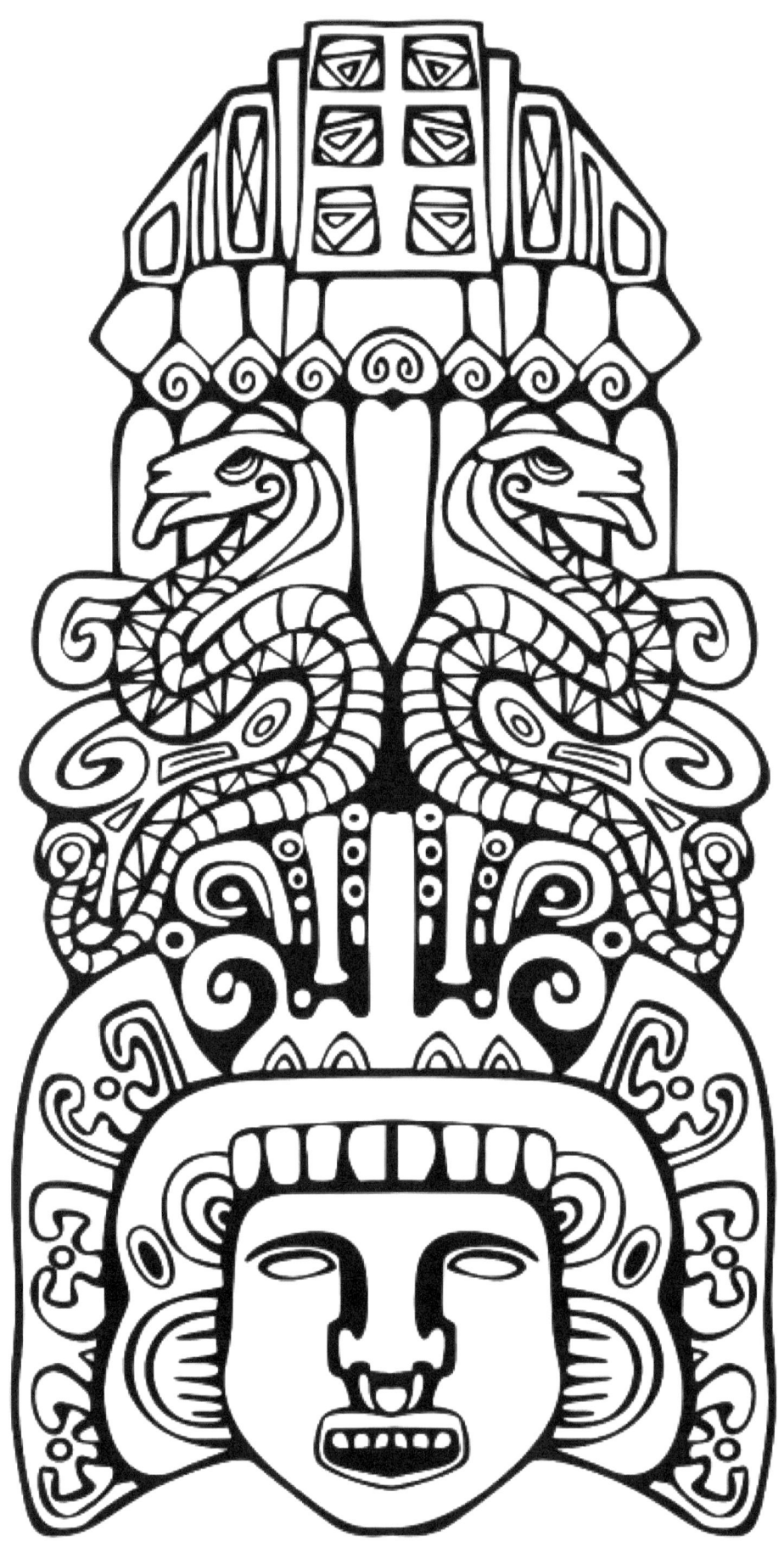

4

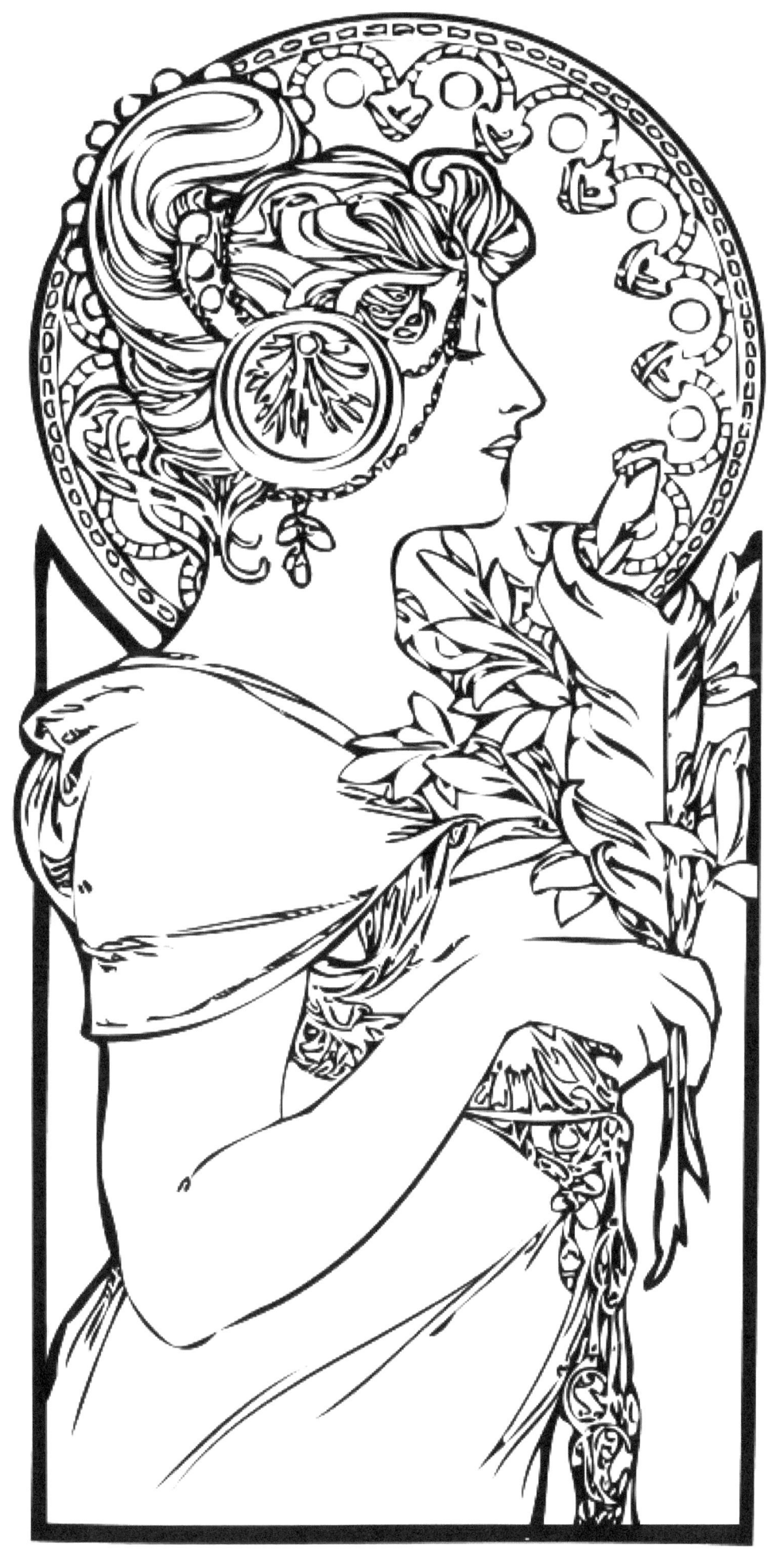

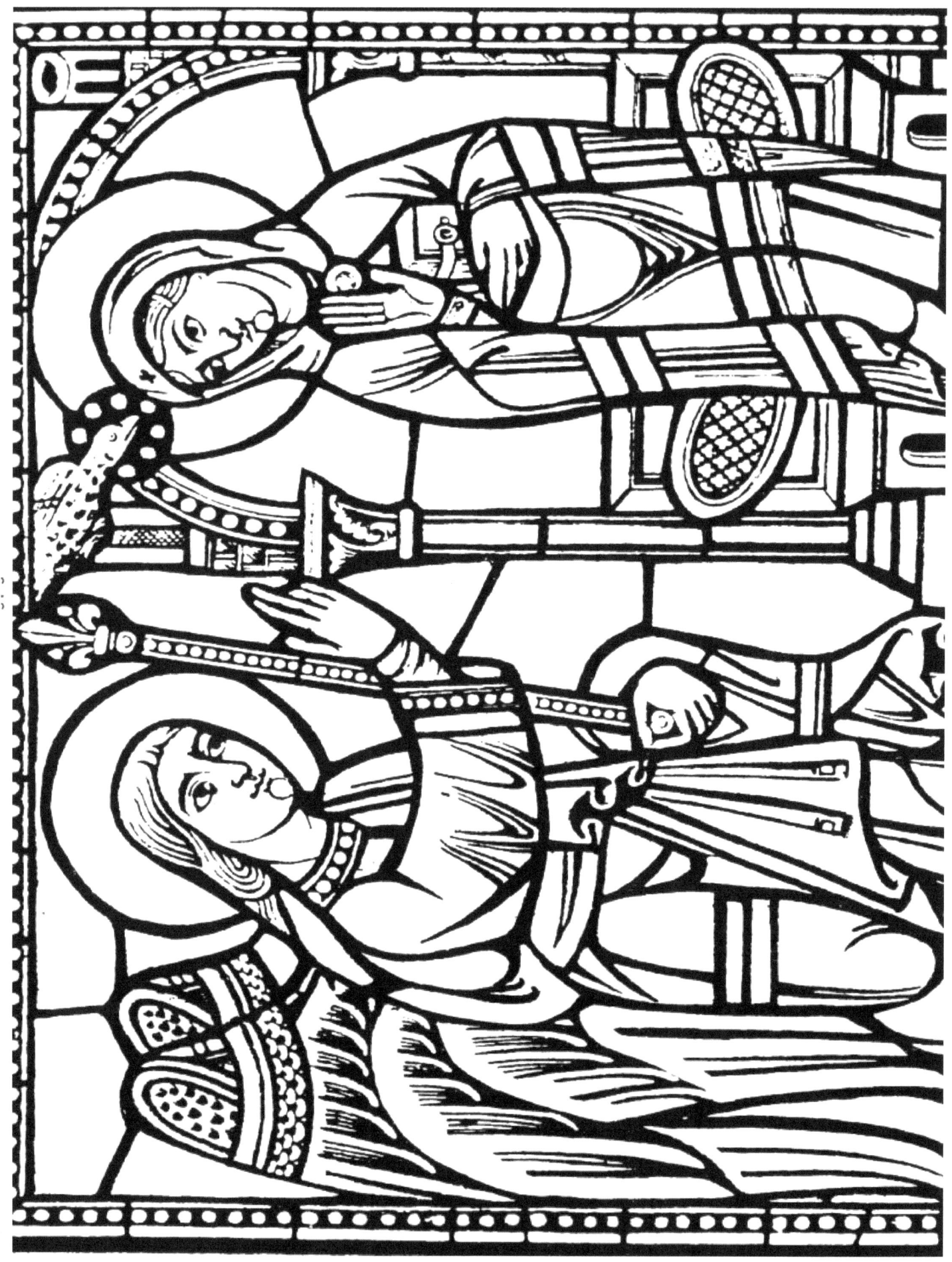

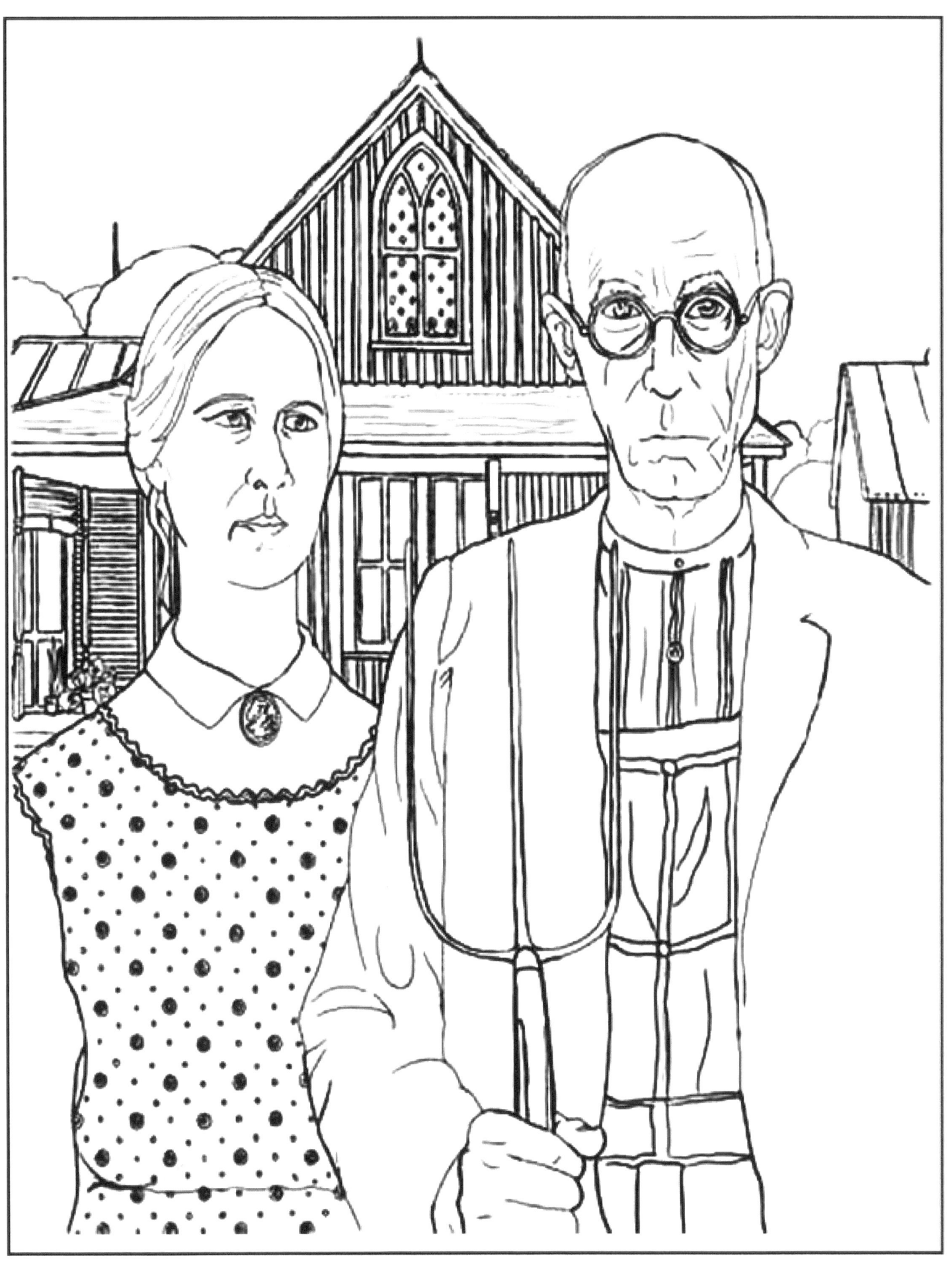

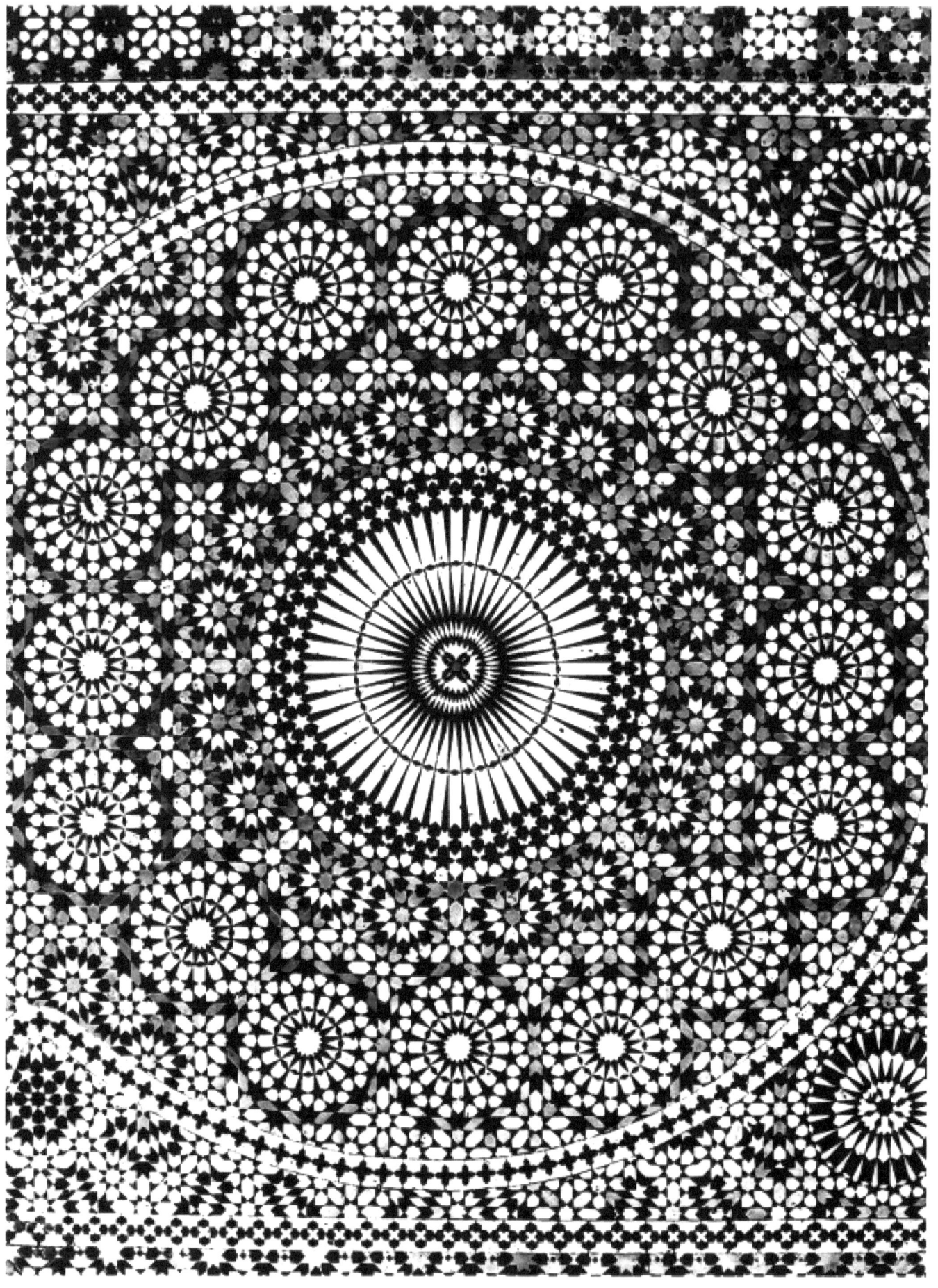

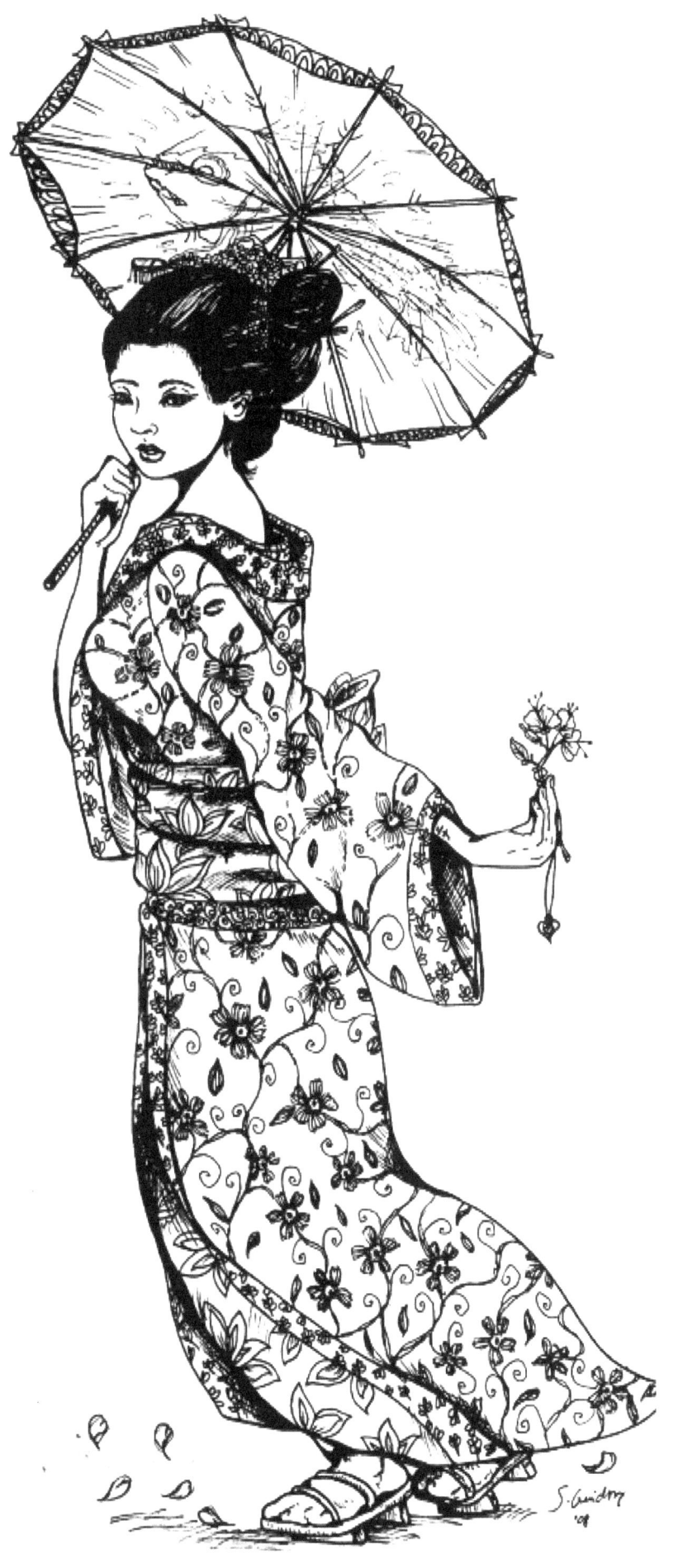

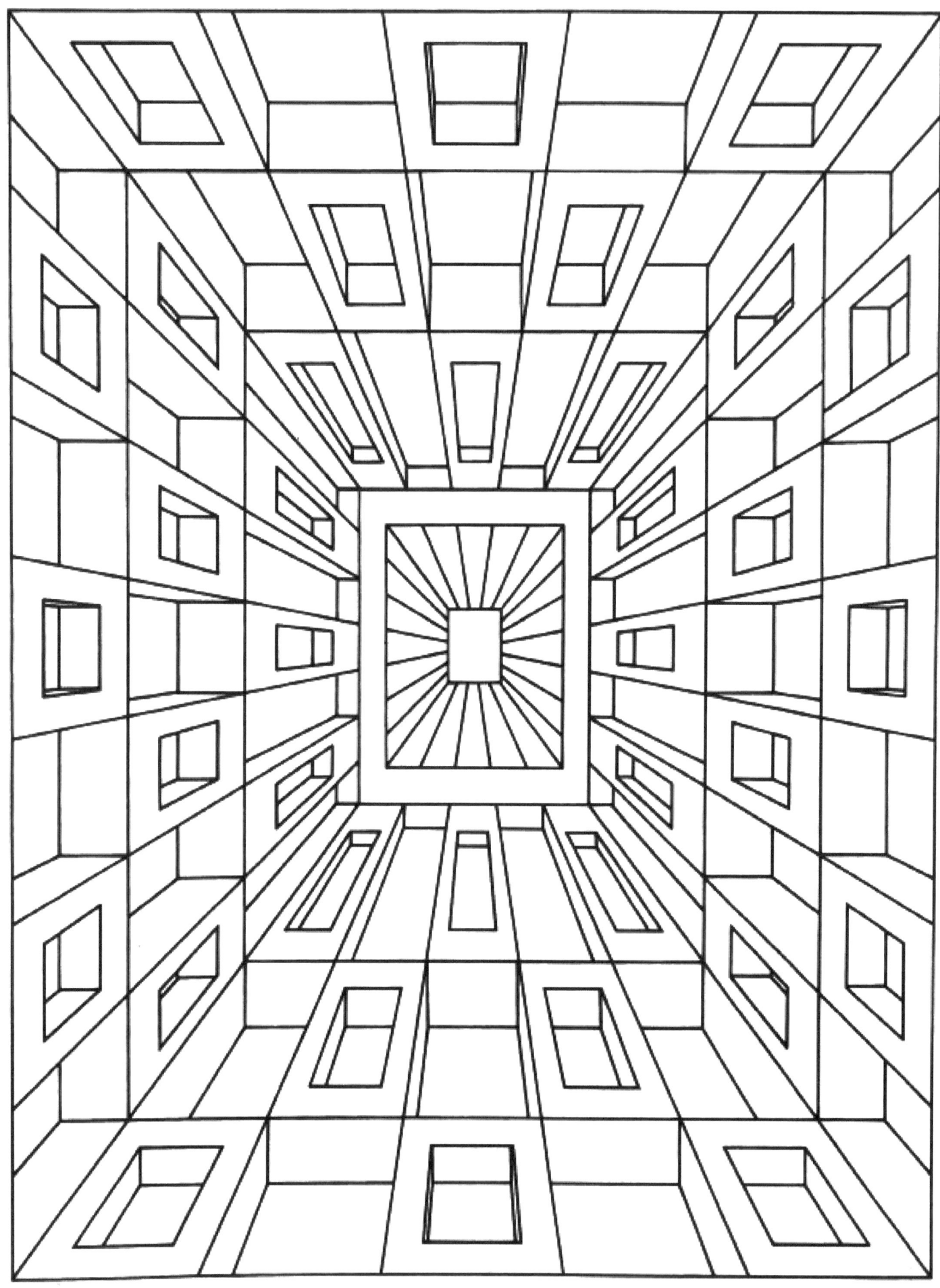

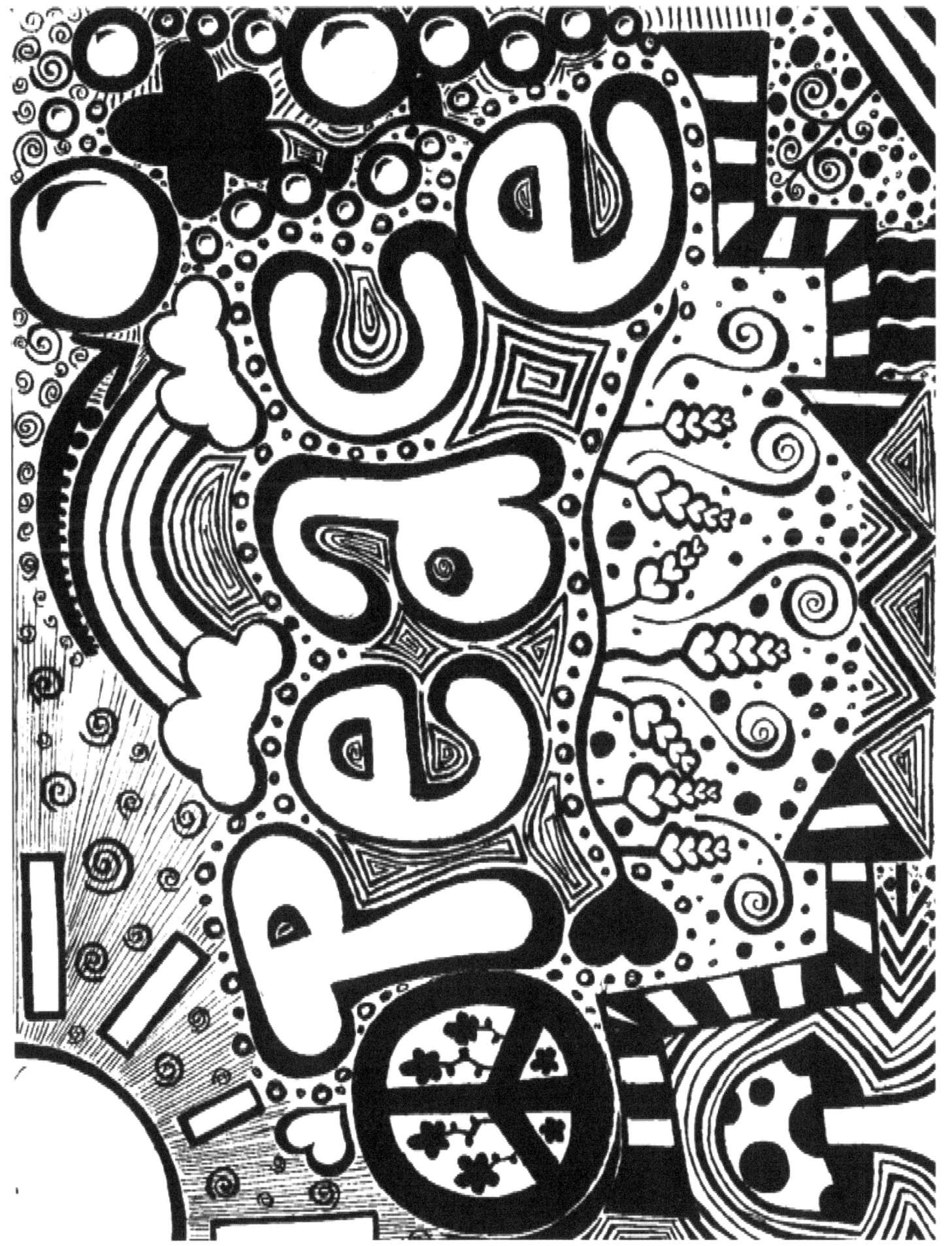

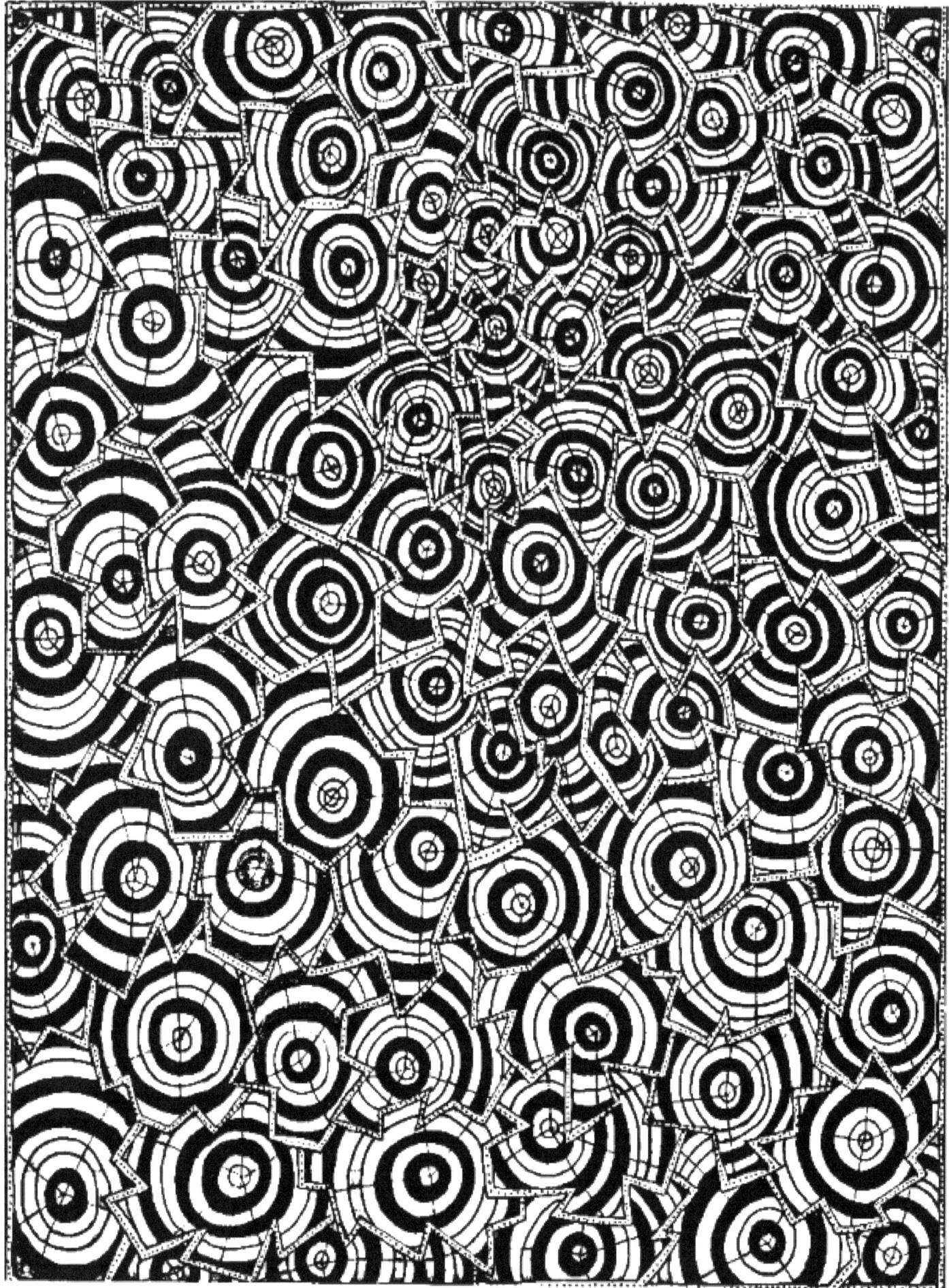

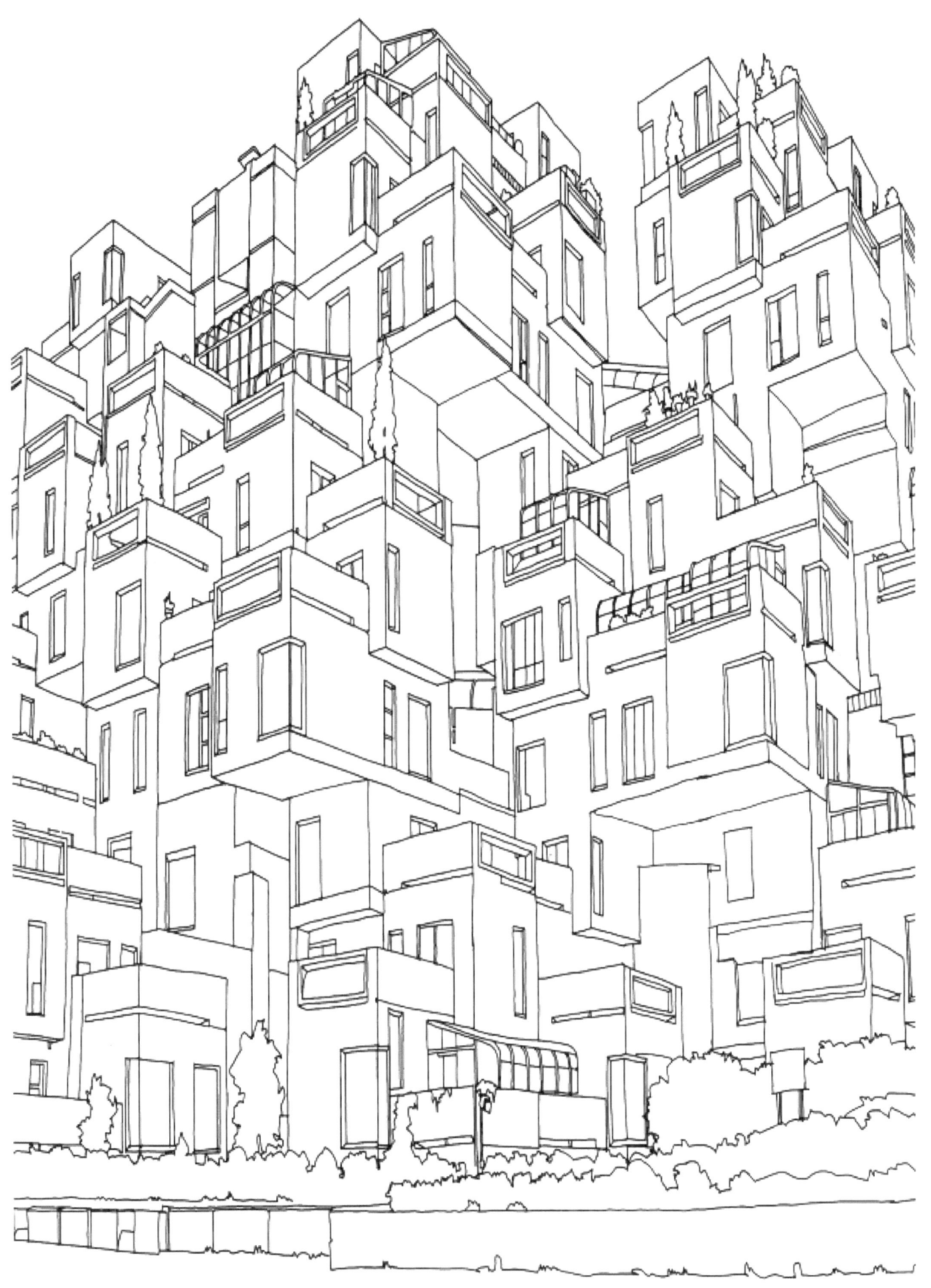

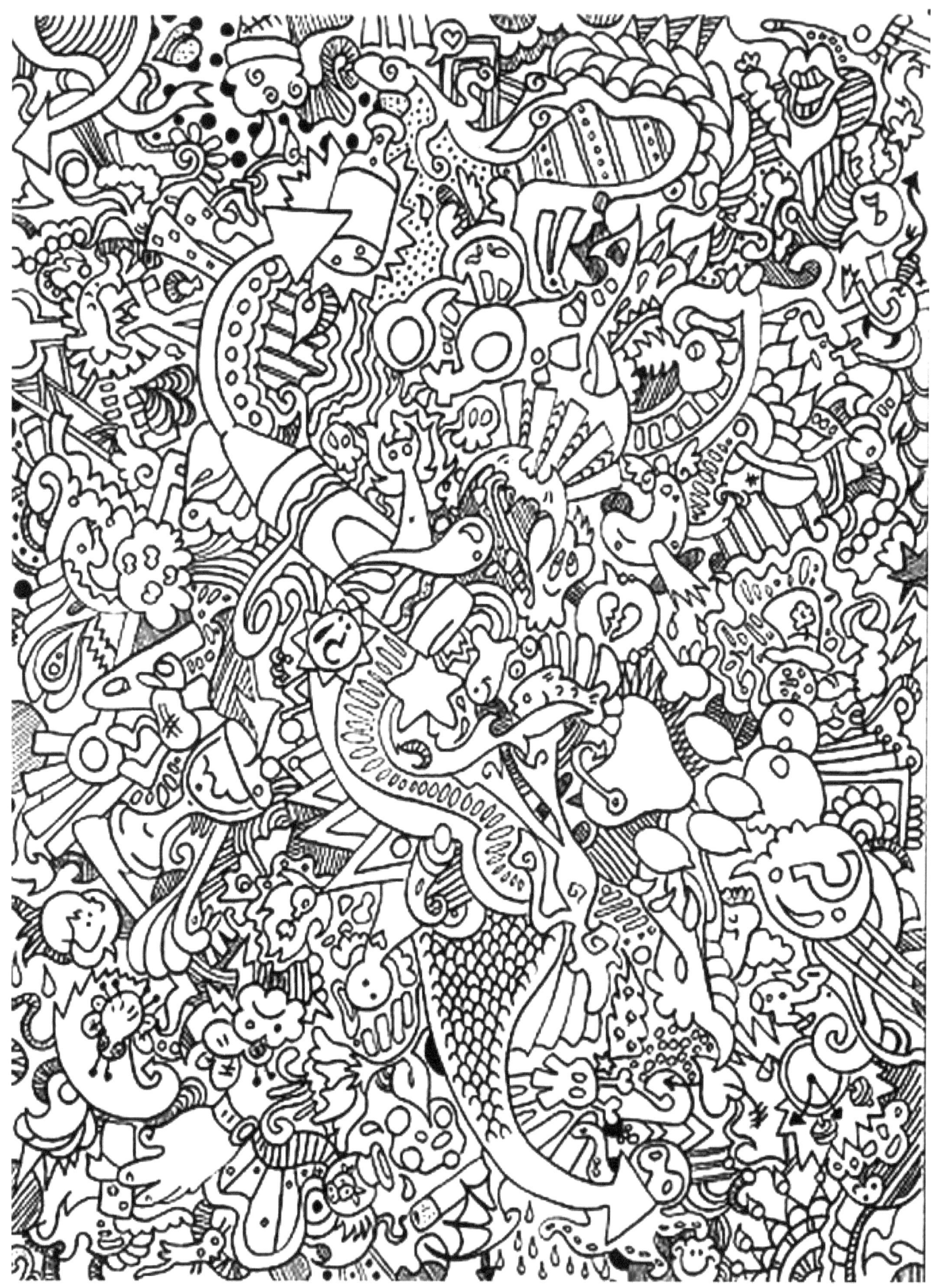

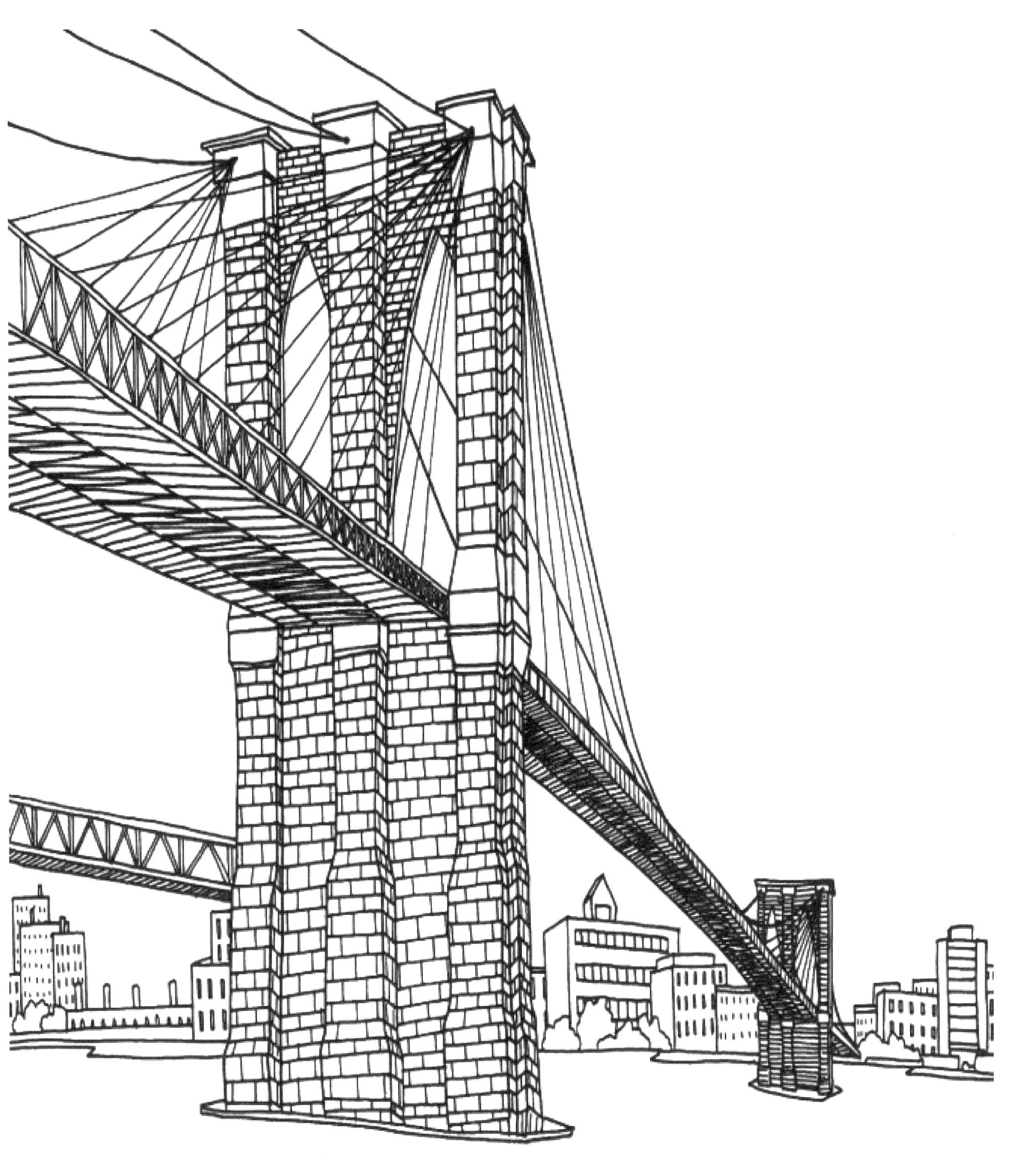

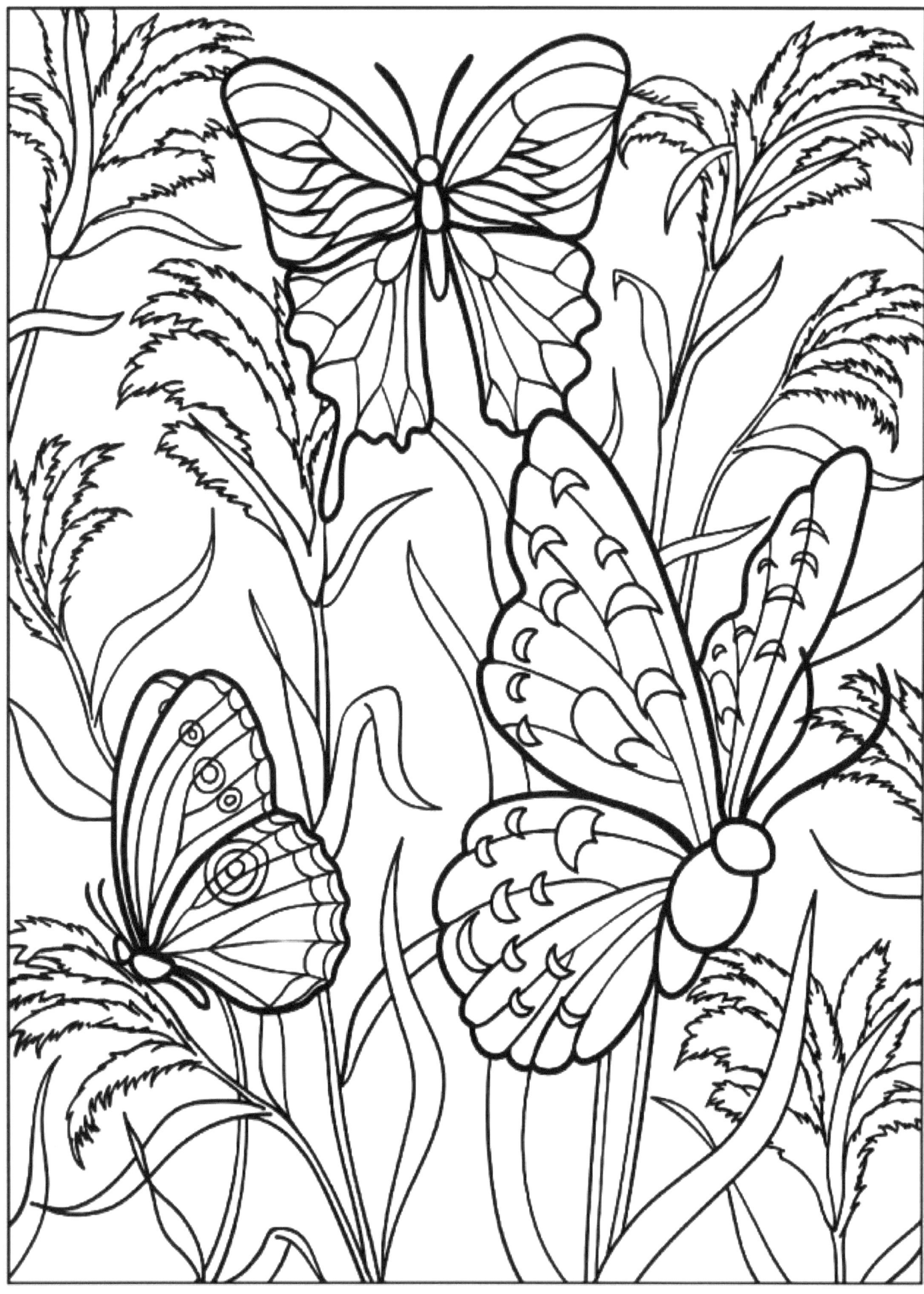

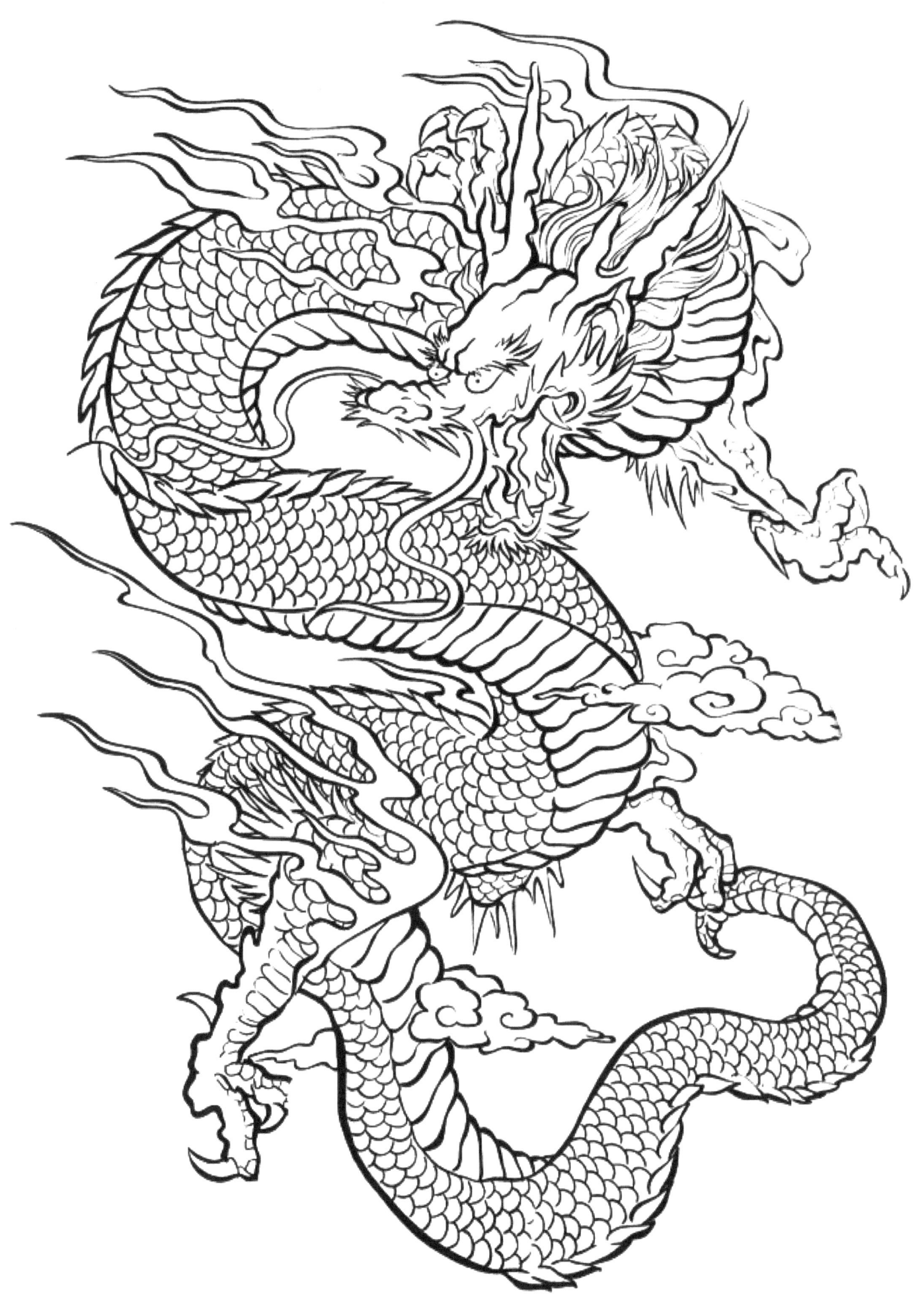

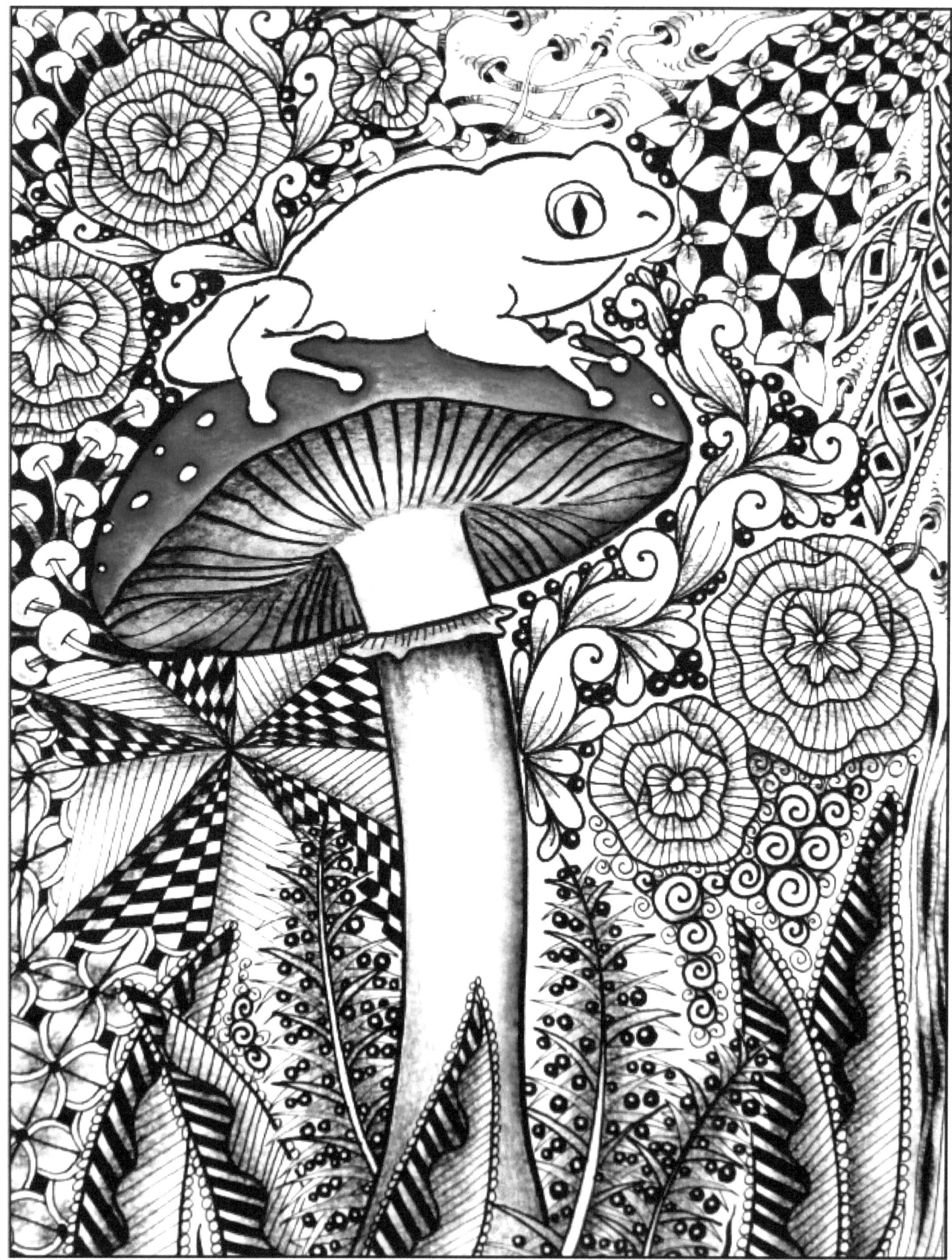

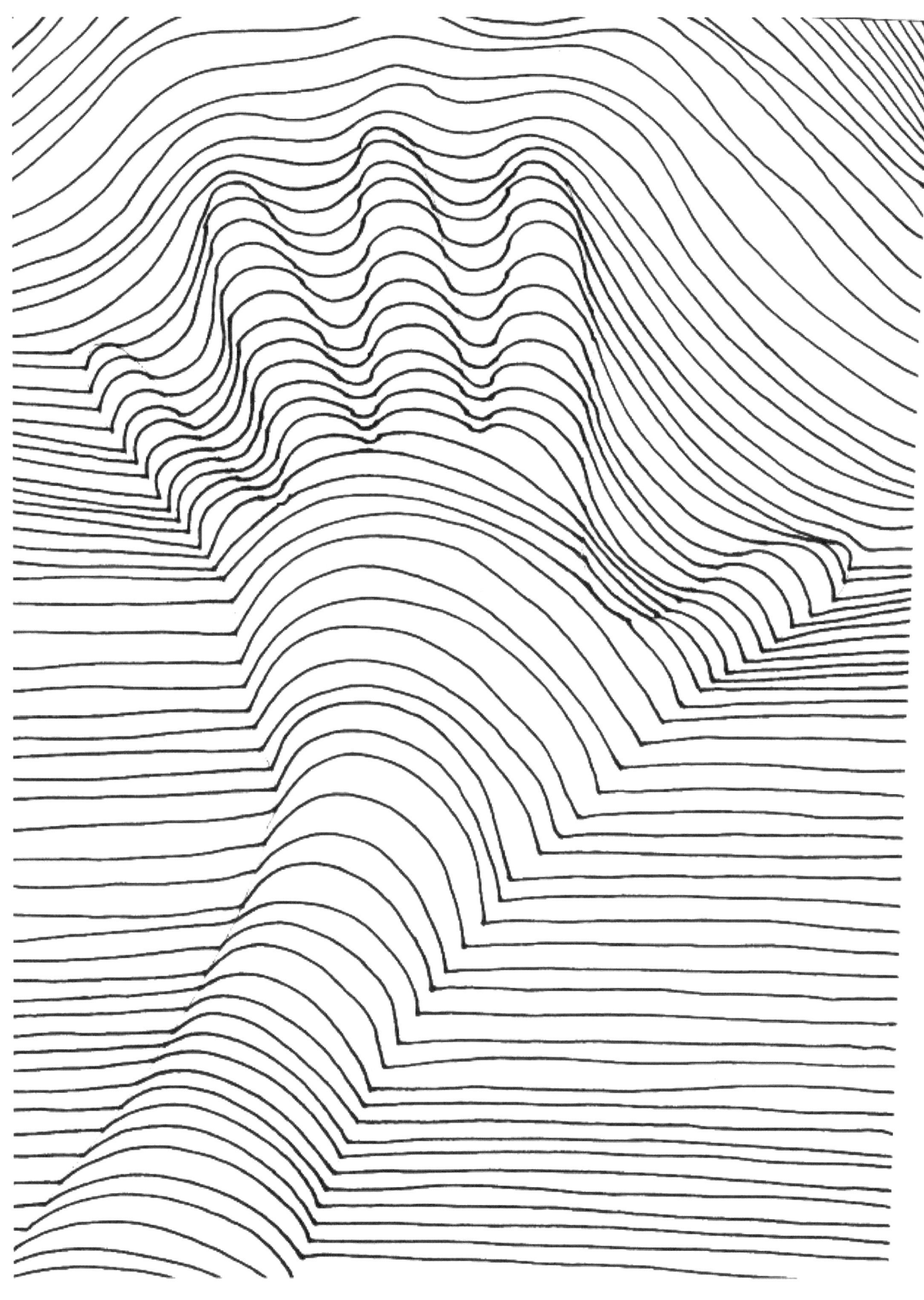

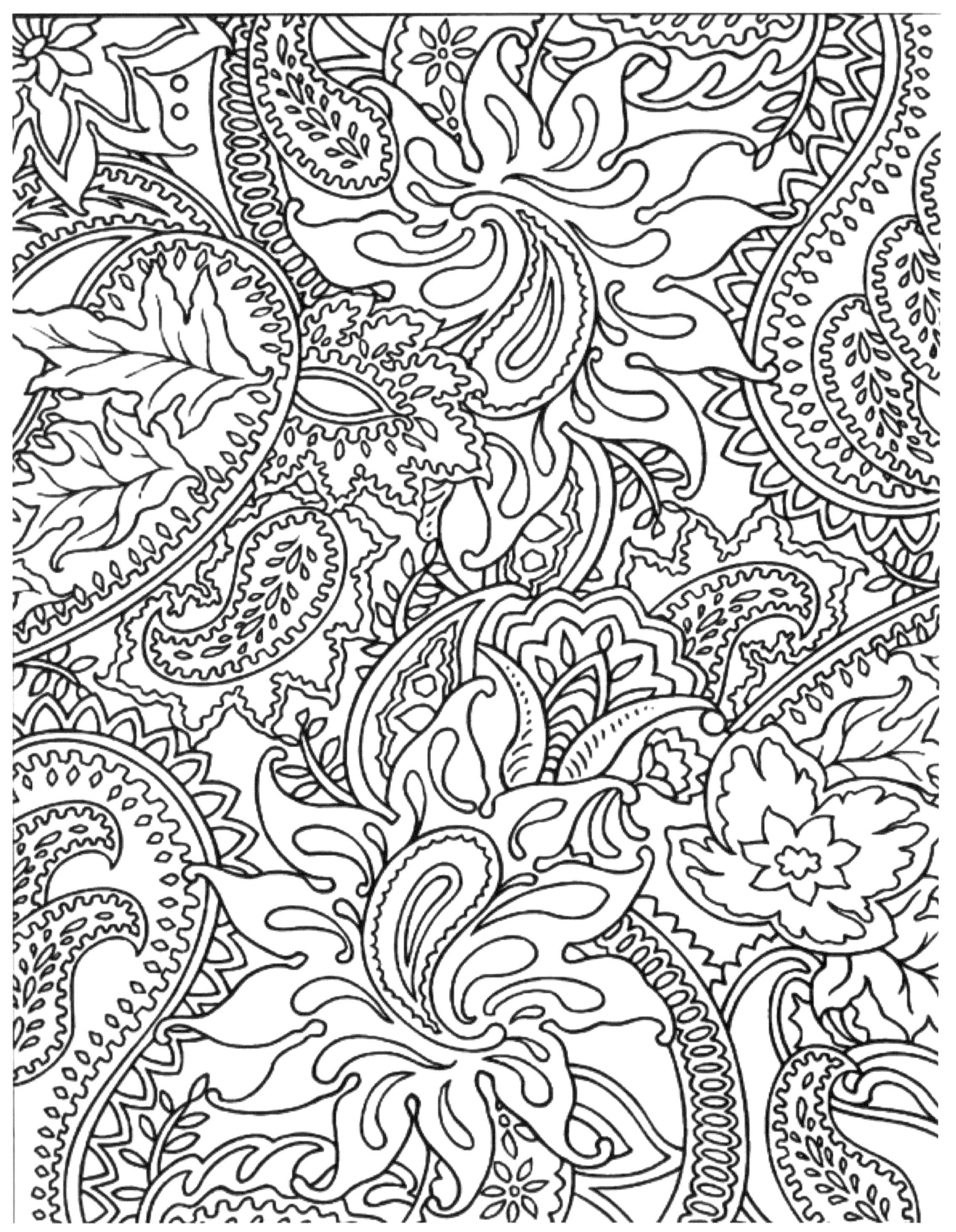

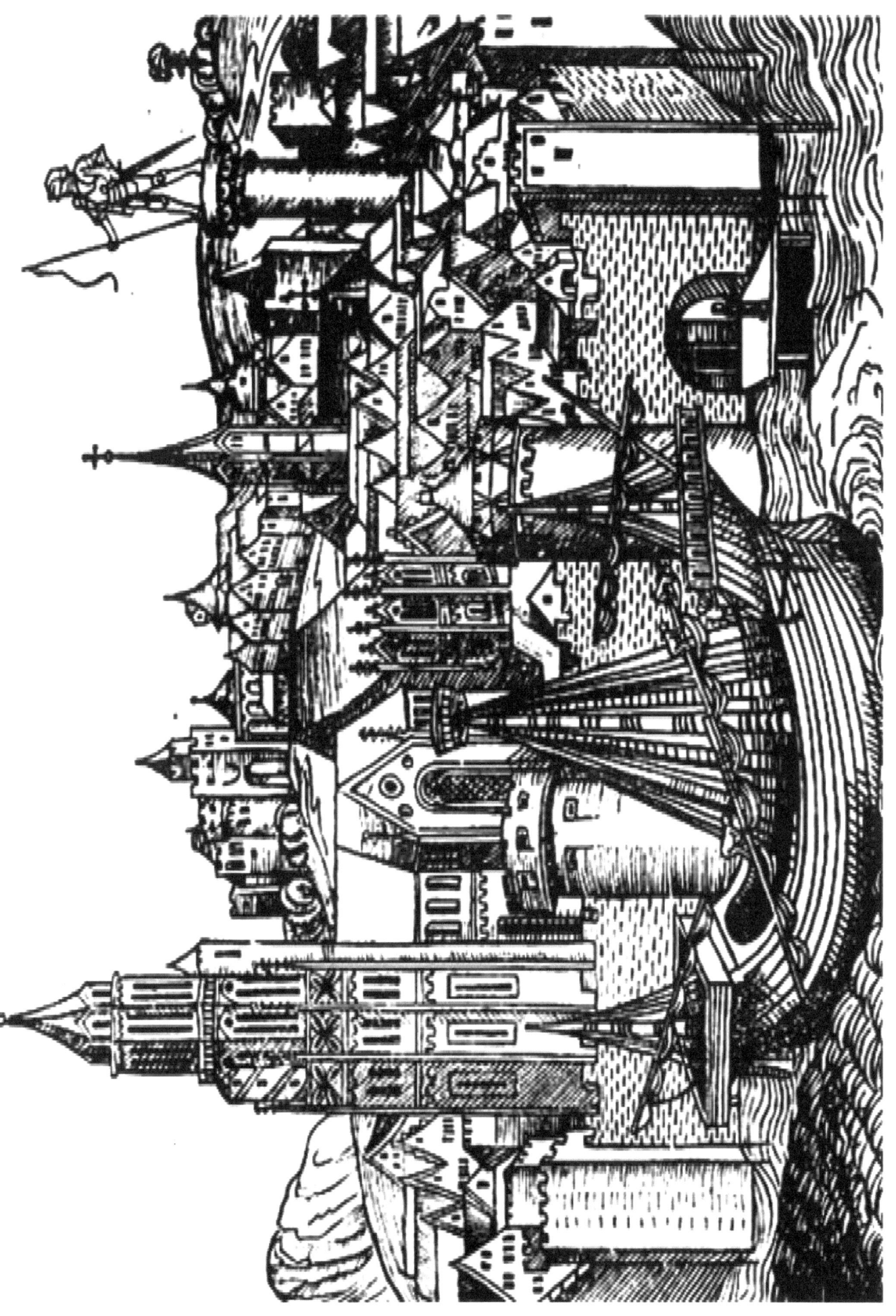

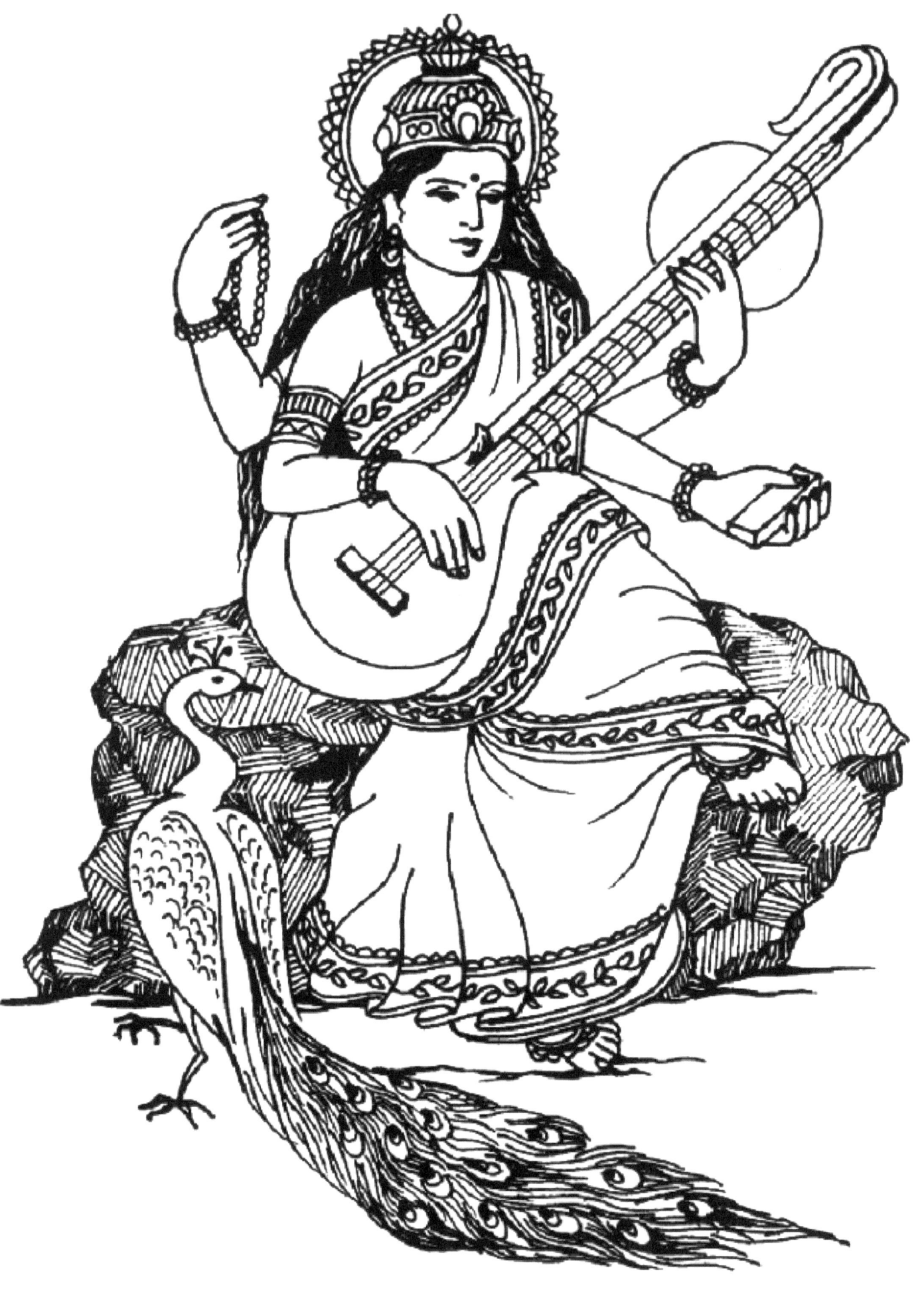

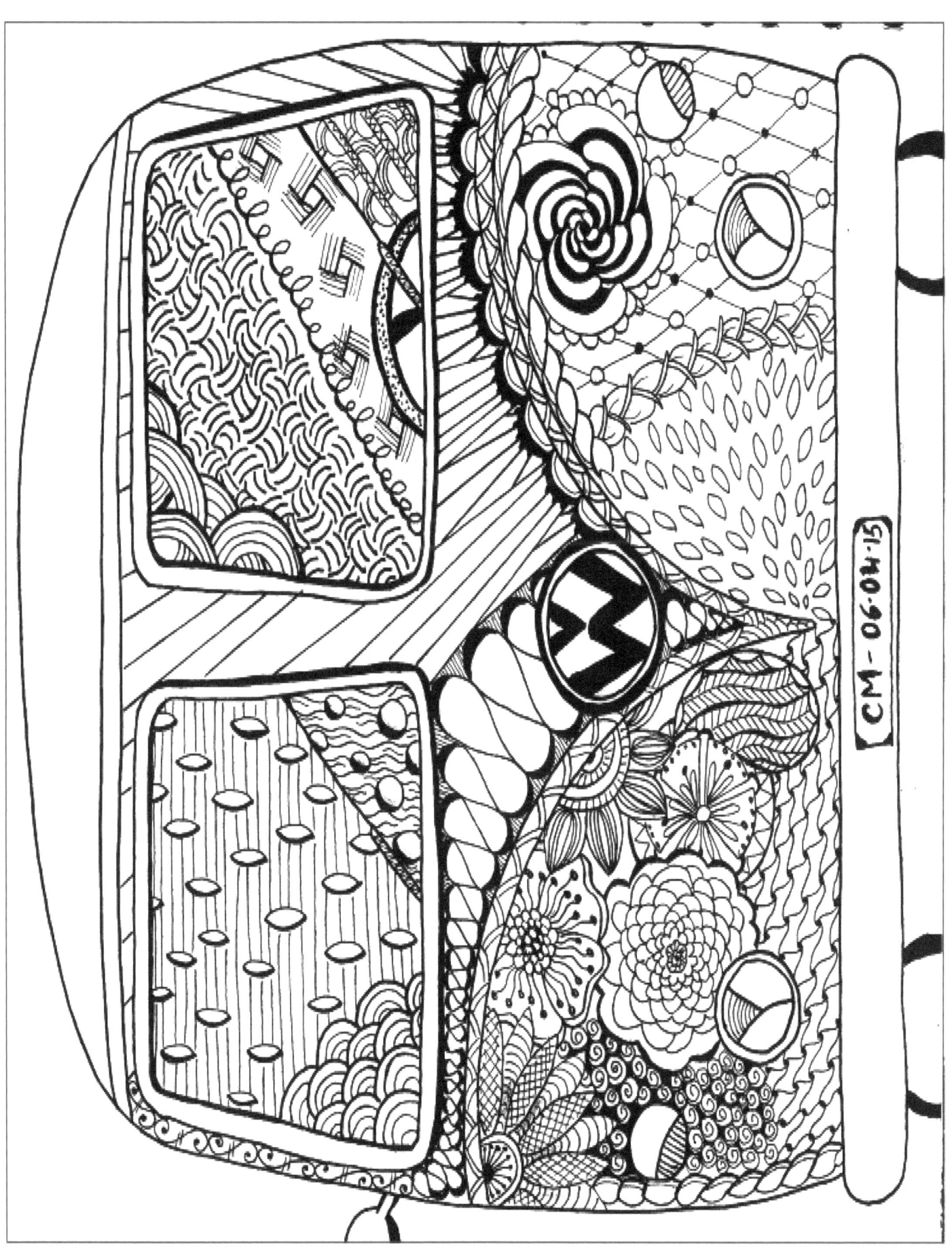

of the above five to attain a new level of peace.

Coloring allows you to unlock your creative potential. Perhaps more important, it helps relieve tension and anxiety.

Be Committed

As with anything in life, if you really want to accomplish something worthwhile, you must be committed to your goal. And if your goal is beating your anxiety, you must START making a real commitment to treatment.

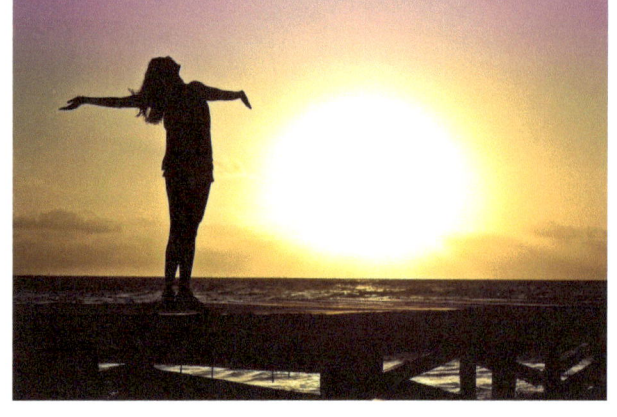

You MUST believe that you can win the battle against anxiety and that a life without its negative effects is really possible for you.

Write this on a big piece of paper – "I WILL Cure My Anxiety." Say it to yourself and stick it on your fridge door, so that you see it daily.

If you have a solid commitment to do whatever it takes to cure your anxiety, you'll recognize failure as only a fork in the road, indicating that you only need to change directions a bit, and try something new.

Make that commitment now and really go for it.

Together we can beat anxiety so you can live the life you deserve.

The Basics of Anxiety

Anxiety symptoms may appear to be random but they're not. Anxiety appears for a reason - stress caused by something happening to you now or by something that happened in the past that you were not able to deal with effectively.

Sources of Anxiety

Those of us who suffer with anxiety have allowed other factors to interfere with normal stress management. Factors like a poor diet, little to no exercise, and insufficient stress relief can all add up to bigger problems. With some simple lifestyle changes, we can easily conquer this form of anxiety.

In addition, ignoring our feelings in stressful situations or trying to bury our emotions about a painful event from the past often lead to the most difficult anxiety symptoms in our lives. This kind of anxiety is a bit harder to overcome. Yet with some help, we can often eliminate those symptoms as well.

The 3 M's of Our Anxiety Cure

Through our blog posts, videos, podcasts, programs and webinars, we'll discuss a host of ways to ease the pain of anxiety today. We refer to our anxiety cure by the three M's:

The first "M" is Mindset. Through our programs, we'll teach you a new way to look at your life and the part anxiety has played in it. This is the "what" of our anxiety cure.

Next is Motivation. By working with us, you'll develop your own positive reasons for moving past anxiety. This is your "why" of curing anxiety.

Finally, Mobilization. You'll create a personalized action plan to live life on your own terms without the painful effects of anxiety. This is the "how" to cure your own anxiety.

Long-Term

A Cure for Anxiety emphasizes how essential it is for individuals to acknowledge to themselves that they are indeed suffering from anxiety. Only by recognizing and acknowledging negative feelings can anxiety be cured.

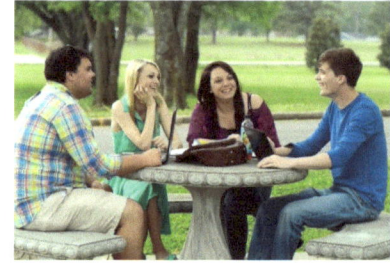

Knowing what caused you to feel stressed and anxious will also help you solve your problems better. Knowing the cause will always lead to the solution.

You don't need to suffer with anxiety. Your anxiety cure starts right here.

You don't have to be alone anymore.